COMMAND LINE BASIC

*programming
in BASIC for
beginners*

Chris Anama-Green

Fourth edition: 2017.

Previously published in 2011 as "Diving into BASIC Computer Programming."

ISBN-10: 1541323262
ISBN-13: 978-1541323261

Table of Contents

Foreword

I originally wrote this book in 2006 because I couldn't find a good command line BASIC programming book when I needed one. I wanted to start out with command line BASIC, as many did, because it's a great way to "stick your toe in the water" without jumping into other programming languages that can be difficult to grasp with no background.

I started computer programming in the late 1990's, and the most recent command line BASIC books I could find were published in the 1970's. Funny enough in retrospect, these command line-driven coding manuals were written as children's picture books.

I also had trouble finding compilers early on: the compilers listed in these books hadn't been around for several decades. Even if I could have gotten my hands on a disk, it probably would have required another piece of antique technology to use.

Today, there are lots of options available for people interested in getting started with coding. For example, the annual *Hour of Code* has enjoyed tremendous success in schools. Many companies offer coding packages for schools that are very user-friendly and offer good exposure for students.

Despite all of the options available now, I still recommend learning how to program in BASIC using a command line interface. It doesn't have to be one's first exposure to coding, but it definitely gives one a greater sense of "raw" power than packaged educational editions.

So, this book is designed to help you learn simple command line BASIC commands. This book contains everything you need to learn BASIC – including instructions for acquiring a free or low-priced compiler/interpreter (see Chapter 1).

BASIC has always been one of the most popular programming languages for people of all ages (including children). Few other programming languages combine the power and ease of use that BASIC provides.

Despite the fact that you'll be learning command line BASIC in this book, BASIC is not "old and outdated." Although the version of BASIC you're learning in this book is not commonly used in commercial applications, its siblings (Visual BASIC, Xojo, and POWERBASIC to name a few) are widely used by everyone from hobbyist programmers to commercial producers of high-quality software.

So if this version of BASIC isn't commonly used commercially, why bother learning it? Well...we all have to start somewhere. I recommend using the knowledge that you gain from this book as a foundation on which you will build a more complex understanding of a more modern form of the BASIC language. Most people don't dive into complex programming without first having at least some knowledge of a simple programming language, like BASIC.

After learning BASIC with this book, you'll be able to write powerful programs in BASIC, move on to other versions of BASIC, or even try your hand at more advanced languages. Or, perhaps you'll be able to rekindle some of the fun and magic that you felt as a child of the 80's programming in BASIC for the first time.

As long as you feel that you've learned something by the end of this book and had fun doing it, you're on the right track.

Let's get started…command line BASIC awaits!

Chris Anama-Green

Chapter 1
BASIC...the Basics

Welcome to Command Line BASIC! I'd first like to start off with a little history and a few terms, and then in no time we'll be on our way to programming in BASIC.

History
BASIC (Beginner's All-purpose Symbolic Instruction Code), hence the name, was designed to be a simple, easily accessible programming language for people of all ages. Created by two Dartmouth Professors in the early 1960's, BASIC became widely popular in the 1980's, when personal computers first became common in homes. BASIC interpreters and compilers were often packaged and included with home computer purchases around this time.

Today, BASIC comes in many varieties and computer users can program in BASIC on all major operating systems including Windows, Mac OS, and Linux as well as mobile applications (yes – you too can create BASIC apps on your iPhone).

But that's enough history for now. Let's get started with some BASIC programming terms!

Terms

Before we dive in, there are a few BASIC programming terms you should be familiar with, as I'll be using them mercilessly in later chapters. You can always refer back here as needed.

An <u>interpreter</u> takes BASIC code that you write and turns it into language that the computer can understand, allowing your program to run. Interpreters do not provide the ability to create stand-alone programs that you can share with others.

A <u>compiler</u>, like an interpreter, takes BASIC code that you write and turns it into a language that the computer can understand. Originally, compilers strictly provided the ability to create programs that easily could be shared with others - without sharing your BASIC code, but they did not run programs, thus creating a need for interpreters. Today, though, *most* compilers also can be used as interpreters.

A <u>command</u> or <u>code</u> can be a single word or a short phrase that tells the computer program what to do. Computer programs are nothing more than a series of commands.

To <u>run</u> a program means to start your program (generally at the beginning of your code). Think of it in terms of a DVD player or iPod. The movie or music file is your program, the DVD player or iPod is your compiler. When you want to run the program, you press play on the DVD player or iPod. Likewise, when you want to see your program in action on your computer, you choose run.

To execute a program means the same thing as to run a program.

An application is another word for a computer program.

To declare a variable means to tell the application what you want the variable to be. Variable data (you'll learn the definition of a variable later on) can be declared by the program or by a user.

Bugs are errors in your program that prevent it from working properly (or from running at all). They're generally typos and sometimes require a lot of feverish searching to find! Most of the programs I reference in this book will do minor debugging, and will tell you which line(s) have a bug.

Choosing Your Compiler or Interpreter

Hundreds of compilers and interpreters are available for whatever operating system your computer is running. Each compiler or interpreter has a slightly different variation of BASIC. That's because BASIC is no longer a universal language. Needless to say, this sometimes makes choosing a compiler/interpreter rather problematic.

For simplicity's sake, I'm assuming you're running Windows, Mac OS, Linux, or iOS. I have selected two applications for you to choose from while using this book. When you complete this book, you can choose another compiler, if you'd like. I'll recommend some at the end of the book. If you're feeling bold and daring, go ahead and pick out a different BASIC compiler or interpreter of your choosing.

Windows Users

FirstBasic | *Compiler*
Though no longer available on PowerBasic's website, you can locate FirstBasic with a simple Google search. FirstBasic is shareware, but is fully functional in the trial version.

Chipmunk Basic | *Interpreter*
Chipmunk Basic is an excellent interpreter, and completely free, to top it all. I recommend downloading it to get a better idea of the difference between compilers and interpreters. To download Chipmunk Basic, go to this website: (http://www.nicholson.com/rhn/basic/) and choose the appropriate version for your operating system.

Mac OS/Linux/iOS Users

Although I know of excellent free compilers for you folks, I'm not recommending them for use with this book because the variations in code are too great.

Chipmunk BASIC | *Interpreter*

I'm recommending that Mac/Linux/iOS users use Chipmunk Basic, with this book. To download Chipmunk Basic, go to this website: (http://www.nicholson.com/rhn/basic/) and choose the appropriate version for your operating system. iOS users can purchase HotPaw BASIC (iOS version of Chipmunk Basic) through the Apple iOS App Store.

METAL BASIC | *Compiler*

I recommend METAL Basic for Mac *after you've used Chipmunk BASIC*. METAL is a powerful compiler and includes several features that are different from the code used in this book (file input/output is an example). You will enjoy using METAL after you are comfortable using BASIC.

Getting Acquainted with the Interface

You'll notice that both programs I recommended for Windows are in DOS – command line. (Mac: Chipmunk Basic is a terminal program.) This may be a different type of program than you're used to.

Neither of the programs is graphical, but rather completely textual. This may intimidate you at first, but you'll soon adjust. Later on you'll be able to use graphical compilers.

You won't be able to use your mouse when working with either of these programs. Thus, navigating in Windows may seem problematic at first - but you'll quickly get used to it! In Windows, simply press F10 when you want to select or unselect the menu (File, Edit, etc.) and use arrow keys (up, down, left, and right) to get what you want! Mac users can use the traditional menu options. Take your time to get used to this new setup to avoid frustration later.

For both applications, if you prefer, you can type your code into a text editor (Notepad, TextEdit, etc.), save it, and open it in the programs. I find that this makes editing code a lot easier.

Line Numbers

You already know the first step of BASIC programming, whether you realize it or not. I'm talking about line numbers. Remember the spelling tests you used to take in elementary school? You always had to number your paper. In BASIC, you do this as well.

Line numbers in BASIC are generally in multiples of 10 (10, 20, 30, 40). This is so that if you forget to insert a line of code, you can easily go back in and add 11 or 25 without having to renumber all of your lines.

When BASIC was first introduced, line numbers were required. The application you are using may or may not require line numbers (some explicitly require line numbers). However, line numbers will be used in most examples found in this book. Use line numbers at least while learning command line BASIC.

PRINT

The easiest BASIC code is the PRINT command. Whenever you want text to show up on the screen, you type:

PRINT "Your Text Goes Here."

Note that PRINT, and all other BASIC commands can be typed in all caps, all lower-case, or a mixture. I type them in all caps in these exercises to make it easier for you to see what I'm doing. Here's an example program, using the PRINT command.

```
10 PRINT "My name is Margaret."
```

Type the above code into your program and run the program. In Chipmunk Basic, type "run" and hit the enter key. In FirstBasic, hit F10 and navigate to the

Run menu, OR simply hit F9. When the program is finished in both applications, simply hit enter.

When you run the program, you should see:

```
My name is Margaret.
```

See how easy that is? If you can do that, you can be a programmer!

END

There are two ways to end a program. First, when running a program from a compiler or interpreter, a program will end itself (but the text will stay on the screen) when there are no more lines of code to read.

Second, you can use the END command to specify when an application ends. When you use the END command, the RUN window closes, so if there is text you'd like the user to read, don't use the END command. Do not use the END command until later in the book. For now, just be familiar with it.

```
10 PRINT "My name is James."
END
```

When you run this program, you won't have time to see the text "My name is James."

Short App:

Write an application using what you've learned in this chapter to say "Hello World!" An example application is below, but see if you can do it on your own first!

```
10 PRINT "Hello World!"
```

Debug Me!

At the end of each chapter you'll find a debugging exercise. The only way to get good at debugging is to practice! See if you can figure out why the program below won't run properly:

```
10 PR1NT "My name is Bob."
EDN
```

Explanation:

Line 10: A simple typo has resulted in a 1 being typed instead of I in "PRINT."

END command: The n and d have been reversed, resulting in "Edn" instead of "End." Also, because the END command is in this application, you won't get to see "My name is Bob." The application will end too quickly.

Moral of the Story: Always check for typos and correct spelling, and remember when to let the program end itself.

Chapter 2
Variables: Virtual weather

Congratulations on making it through the first chapter! Now that you have a few basics down, we can work on creating applications that really do something.

CLS
CLS is a simple, yet powerful command. CLS simply means "clear screen." It's good practice to get into the habit of putting CLS at the very beginning of every application. Doing this will remove any text left from the last time you ran the program. It leaves you with a clean screen free of distractions.

Additionally, CLS can be used **anytime** you'd like a fresh screen - not just at the beginning of the program. Because all text will be erased, you may want to "re-print" necessary text after CLS.

CLS may seem a bit confusing now, but after you've completed this chapter its purpose should make perfect sense.

Here's an example:

```
CLS
10 PRINT "Hello computer user!"
CLS
10 PRINT "Sup?"
```

This code produces:

```
Sup?
```

Notice that although "Hello computer user!" is printed, the screen is cleared before you can see it, so all you will see is "Sup?"

Variables

Let's talk about variables! A variable is nothing more than a little data temporarily stored in your computer's memory by the program. Variable data is cleared from your system every time the program ends (you'll learn how to make the computer "remember" variables in another chapter).

There are many types of data and thus many types of variables. For our purposes, we're going to pretend that there are two types of data: Numerical (Integers) and Strings.

You may remember from elementary school math that an **integer** is a number that can be positive, negative, or zero. In BASIC, integers can be added, subtracted, multiplied, and divided (among other things). You'll learn about this later, but for now - it's just important that you recognize what an integer is!

Strings can be single words or complete sentences. There is a limit to how much data strings can hold (254 characters), so don't get too long-winded for one string! BASIC string data CANNOT contain commas (,) or quotation marks ("). Including such characters will royally destroy string data – and your program!

Naming variables is important. The names you assign to variables will tell the computer what type of data the variable contains, and therefore, how to handle the data.

A numerical (integer) variable is generally named with a single letter. In *some* compilers/interpreters, the letter is case sensitive. (A is not the same thing as a.) In FirstBasic and Chipmunk Basic, though variable names are not case sensitive. (A is the same as a.) You should get into the habit of using A OR a, and not both in the same application.

A string variable is generally named with a single letter followed by $ (the $ denotes that the variable is a string). String variable names can, however, include multiple letters. CHRI$ is a valid variable string name, as is A$. String variables have the same case sensitivity (or lack thereof) rules as numerical variables.

Using Variables

To set a STRING variable equal to something, simply type the variable name, followed by = and the data in quotation marks.

```
A$="My name is Chris Anama-Green."
```

To set a NUMERICAL variable equal to something, type the variable name, followed by = and the integer, but do not include quotation marks.

```
N=78
```

You can set variables equal to each other by putting the variable you'd like to change first, and the variable whose value you'd like the first variable to assume after the equal sign. More simply: think of the first variable as the empty basket (even if it already has data), and the second as the full basket "sharing" its data with the first basket.

```
A=50
B=25
A=B
```

Now, A is no longer 50, but is now 25. B does not change.

Getting Variable Data from the User

You now (hopefully) know how to assign values to variables, but what if you want to collect data for variables from the user? It's simpler than you might think.

Use the INPUT command followed by the variable name for which you'd like data. If you put a variable name after INPUT for a variable that already has data, the data already stored by that variable will be erased and replaced by the new user entered data. Here's an example:

```
CLS
10 PRINT "Hello! How are you today?"
20 INPUT B$
END
```

This code produces:

```
Hello! How are you today?
?
```

Using User Input

So, what good is user input if you can't use it? There are several ways to use and manipulate user input, and you're about to learn the first.

You can print user input right onto the screen using the PRINT command, followed by the variable you'd like to print.

```
CLS
10   PRINT   "What   is   your   favorite
number?"
20 INPUT C
30 PRINT "You said:"
40 PRINT C
```

This app looks like:

```
What is your favorite number?
? (6)
You said:
6
```

You can print your text AND the user's input on the same line by simply adding a semicolon (;) between the two.

22

Example:

```
CLS
10 PRINT "What is your favorite
number?"
20 INPUT C
30 PRINT "You said: " ; C ; "!"
```

The revised application looks like:

```
What is your favorite number?
? (50)
You said: 50!
```

Comments

It's been an intense chapter, but you stuck through 'til the end! There's one last thing I'd like you to learn before I set you free: how to add comments to BASIC code.

You can probably already tell that after you get lots and lots of lines of BASIC code, it could become difficult for you to remember what everything is supposed to do. This is especially true when you're using hundreds of variables! Not to worry, you can make notes for yourself by using comments.

Simply put an apostrophe (') at the beginning of each comment line, and your compiler or interpreter will ignore it. For now, comments have to be on lines of their own.

```
'This clears the screen
CLS
10 PRINT "Hello friend! What is your
name?"
20 INPUT A$
'The above variable stores the user's
name
30 PRINT "Nice to see you again " ; A$
'The code below ends the program
```

Comments don't show up when you run the program:

```
Hello friend! What is your name?
? (Agatha)
Nice to see you again, Agatha!
```

Short App:

I'd like for you to write an application that greets a user by name and then asks for the person's age. Try it on your own first, using what you've learned in this chapter. If you get stuck, I've written an example application for you.

```
CLS
10 PRINT "Welcome to my humble abode.
Your name?"
'T$ Stores name
20 INPUT T$
30 PRINT "Hello "; T$ ;". How old are
you?"
'Z Stores age
40 INPUT Z
50 PRINT Z; " is a good age to be."
```

Debug Me!

See if you can find the bugs in the below application!

```
CLS
10 PRINT "What state are you from?"
20 INPUT G$
30 PRINT "Is "= GS ;" a nice place to
live?"
30 INPUT $H
```

Explanation:

Line 30: an equal sign (=) has accidentally been inserted instead of a semicolon (;). GS has been entered instead of G$. No GS variable has been declared in this application.

Line 40: Line 40 has been mislabeled as "30." Two line 30's cannot exist in the same application. H$ has been mistyped as $H.

Moral of the Story: Always double check variable names, symbols, and line numbers.

Chapter 3
IF It's Hot *THEN* I Melt

COLOR

The COLOR command works only with Windows, and more specifically only in FirstBasic. (The COLOR command also works with other BASIC compilers/interpreters for Windows - Chipmunk BASIC just isn't one of them.) If you're on a Mac or Linux - just skip ahead.

As you might expect, the COLOR command changes text color. To use this command, simply type COLOR followed by the appropriate number of the color you'd like your text to be.

COLOR 8

You have 16 colors to choose from including:

Black	**0**	Gray	**8**
Dark Blue	**1**	Blue	**9**
Dark Green	**2**	Green	**10**
Dark Aqua	**3**	Aqua	**11**
Dark Red	**4**	Red	**12**
Dark Magenta	**5**	Magenta	**13**
Brown	**6**	Yellow	**14**
Light Gray	**7**	White	**15**

Here's code for an application that uses COLOR.

```
CLS
10 COLOR 15
20 PRINT "Now I'm white!"
30 COLOR 10
40 PRINT "Now I'm green!"
```

And the application when you run it:

```
Now I'm white!
Now I'm green!
```

GOTO

Are you beginning to see how *basic* BASIC really is? If not, the next command should help you see the light. The GOTO command does exactly what it says. It skips ahead directly to the line number that you specify. To use GOTO, simply type GOTO followed by the line number.

GOTO 20

Keep in mind that anything between the GOTO command and the line that it specifies will be skipped - even if you have some really important code there! Be sure to plan ahead.

```
CLS
10 PRINT "Now I'm going to line 50!"
20 GOTO 50
30 PRINT "Skip me!"
40 PRINT "Skip me too!"
50 PRINT "WOOHOO! I made it to line 50!"
```

When you run it, your application should look like this:

```
Now I'm going to line 50!
WOOHOO! I made it to line 50!
```

So this GOTO business is all well and good, but how the heck is it useful if it just skips lines? You're about to find out.

IF...THEN

The IF...THEN command is about to become your best friend. IF...THEN simply means that IF "such and such" is true, THEN "this and that" happens. Here's an example in English: IF you stay up too late THEN you will be tired in the morning.

IF...THEN is used with variables and another command of your choosing, most commonly

PRINT or GOTO. (But really, you can even use COLOR if you so choose.) Here's what an IF...THEN statement looks like:

```
IF F$="yes" THEN PRINT "I'm glad you
said yes!"
```

Another example, using a numerical variable:

```
IF H=1 THEN GOTO 70
```

Multiple IF...THEN statements combined become very useful - especially when you're providing the user with multiple options (kind of like a 1-800 number: press 1 for English, 2 for Español, 3 for Français...you get the picture.)

```
IF A$="1" THEN GOTO 50
IF A$="2" THEN GOTO 70
IF A$="3" THEN GOTO 90
```

Keep in mind that the variable, if it's a string, is case sensitive. Therefore, if the user enters "Yes" and your IF...THEN statement says IF G$="yes" the conditions are not met for the IF...THEN statement to go through (i.e. whatever is after THEN won't happen.) Remember this when programming. Here's an example:

```
CLS
10 PRINT "Welcome! What is your name?"
20 INPUT A$
30 PRINT "Welcome " + A$
40 PRINT A$ + " are you older than 18?
(y/n)"
50 INPUT B$
60 IF B$="y" THEN GOTO 80
70 IF B$="n" THEN GOTO 100
80 CLS
85 PRINT "You are older than 18!"
90 GOTO 120
100 CLS
105 PRINT "You are not older than 18!"
110 GOTO 120
120 PRINT "That's all folks!"
```

Naming Sections

In BASIC, you can name sections of code rather than use line numbers. Although I will continue to use line numbers throughout most of the rest of the book, I'd like you to at least have seen this method of programming, as it will be extremely useful to you should you choose to program in another variety of BASIC later. **Note:** sections are not supported by some command line BASIC compilers/interpreters.

To name a function, simply type an alphanumeric name, followed by a colon (:) and press "enter."

Here's an example of code with named functions rather than line numbers.

```
CLS
PRINT "WELCOME! Do you prefer English
or Spanish?"
INPUT L$
IF L$="English" THEN GOTO English
If L$="Spanish" THEN GOTO Spanish

English:
CLS
PRINT "You prefer English!"
GOTO Done

Spanish:
CLS
PRINT "You prefer Spanish!"
GOTO Done

Done:
PRINT "All done! Wasn't that easy?"
```

Note: If you don't have a GOTO or END statement at the end of a section, the interpreter/compiler will continue reading the next lines down. If the English section did not have "GOTO Done" at the end, the application would also go through "Spanish." This would result in "You prefer English!" *AND* "You prefer Spanish!" both being printed.

Short App:

I'd like you to write an application that takes the user to different lines of code depending on gender. An example app is below. Write your own version. You can even include different colors for different genders if you like. Be creative and have fun!

```
CLS
10 PRINT "What is your gender? (m/f)"
20 INPUT X$
30 IF X$="m" THEN GOTO 50
40 IF X$="f" THEN GOTO 80
50 CLS
60 PRINT "You're a boy!"
70 GOTO 110
80 CLS
90 PRINT "You're a girl!"
100 GOTO 110
110 PRINT "You've reached the end...again."
```

Debug Me!

```
CSL
10  PRINT "Do you like pickles? (y/n)"
20  INPUT A
30  IF A="y" then GOTO 41
40  IF A="n" then GOTO 30
50  PRINT "You like pickles!"
60  GOTO 90
70  PRINT "You hate pickles!"
80  GOTO 90
90  "Thank you for completing the
survey."
```

Explanation:

Line 20, 30, 40: A numerical variable is declared, when the type of data we're interested in is string data!

Line 30: The program is instructed to go to a line that does not exist.

Line 40: The program is told to go to line 30. When this happens, the program will go to line 30, then again to line 40, again to line 30, again to line 40, and well...you get the picture. This is called an "infinite loop." While infinite loops are fun when you're just messing around with code, they create bugs that keep your programs from functioning normally!

Moral of the Story: Always check variable data types, double check the line number after GOTO, and avoid infinite loops!

Chapter 4

Good Input=Good Data

Getting Input from a File

You already know how to get input from users, but did you know that you can also get input from a file stored on the computer?

First, it's important that you either: know the full path to the file on the computer, or that you store the file in the same folder as the compiler, interpreter, or compiled program.

For example, in Windows the full path could be "C:\filename.txt" or "C:\program files\chipmunk basic\filename.txt". However, I find it much easier to simply store the file in the same folder as the compiler, interpreter, or compiled program. To do this, the file path would simply be "filename.txt"

Now, before you can input from a file, the file must exist to get input from. It's possible to create files with BASIC, but we'll get into that in the next chapter. It may seem like a no-brainer, but make sure you create the file before you attempt to input from it.

Let's try an example. First, create a file in the location of your choice, but make sure to get the correct path name. You also should open the file and type something in on the first line, perhaps your name, then save and close it. The code is as follows:

```
OPEN "filename.txt" FOR INPUT AS #1
INPUT #1, A$
CLOSE
```

That's the code! These three lines open a file, get input from the file, and close the file. Let's take a closer look. You see #1 in two places. This refers to the file number that you have opened. That means you can have multiple files open at once. Just repeat the code and change the number (and, of course, variable) to open another file simultaneously.

The A$ after #1 assigns the variable name A$ to the information that you inputted from the file.

After you're completely finished inputting from the file, you must CLOSE the file.

Displaying Input

You now know how to input data from a file, but how do you display inputted data? Well, after your inputted data has a variable name, you can treat it like any other variable! Here's a bit of sample code:

```
CLS
10 PRINT "I'm opening a file now..."
20 OPEN "yourfilenamehere.txt" for input as #1
30 INPUT #1, A$
31 CLOSE
40 PRINT "Your stored data is: " + A$
50 PRINT "Isn't that cool?"
```

Multiple File Inputs

It's possible to input multiple times from a file. This inputs the first line of the file, second line, third line, and so on - as many inputs as you put. Be careful not to attempt to input a line that doesn't exist (for example: having four inputs when only three lines exist).

You must assign a different variable name to each input event. This is particularly useful for storing different bits of information about a user. For example, you can store a name on the first line, birth date on the second line, and age on the third line.

Now I'd like you to create a new file, put your name on the first line, age on the second line, and favorite color on the third line.

Here's an example:

```
CLS
10 PRINT "I know everything about you:"
20 OPEN "userdata.txt" for input as #5
30 INPUT #5, name$
40 INPUT #5, age$
50 INPUT #5, color$
55 CLOSE
60 PRINT "Your name is: " + name$
70 PRINT "Your age is: " + age$
80 PRINT "Your favorite color is: " +
color$ +  "!"
```

Using Inputs from Multiple Files

I briefly mentioned before that you can use input from multiple files. This is very simple, and only requires repeating the commands.

If you'd like to try this, create two different files and enter a bit of data in each.

Here's an example:

```
CLS
10 OPEN "file1.txt" for input as #1
20 INPUT #1, A$
30 CLOSE
40 OPEN "file2.txt" for input as #2
50 INPUT #2, B$
60 CLOSE
70 PRINT "This is input from file 1: "
+ A$
80 PRINT "This is input from file 2: "
+ B$
```

Using File Input to Verify Information

The usefulness of this next example doesn't extend very far beyond its "coolness factor." The example uses a file to store a password. I say that this file input method is not particularly useful because anyone can simply open the file, read the password, and type it into the program. Still though, adding passwords to your applications is pretty cool, aye?

Let's skip directly to the example. As usual, create a file, open it, type in a simple password (don't use any of your real passwords for obvious reasons), save it, and close it.

```
CLS
10 OPEN "password.txt" for input as #1
20 INPUT #1, A$
30 CLOSE
40 PRINT "Enter your password!"
50 INPUT B$
60 IF B$=A$ THEN GOTO 90
70 PRINT "Wrong Password!"
80 GOTO 110
90 PRINT "That's right!"
100 GOTO 110
110 PRINT "End of app."
```

Compiling Your Application

So far, I haven't taught you how to compile an application. Mac and Linux users: skip this, because Chipmunk Basic, remember, is an interpreter and does not provide compiling functionality. In Chapter 1 I recommended a compiler for you to use later on.

Windows FirstBasic users: Now that you should be sufficiently comfortable with FirstBasic, you're ready to learn how to compile an application. To do this, first create or open a file to compile. Now press F10 and use the arrow keys to navigate to "Compile." Press enter. Go down to "Destination." Press enter. Use your arrow keys to select "EXE file." Press enter. Press the UP arrow key to select compile. Press enter. The exe file will be compiled in the same directory as the source file.

Short App

I'd like you to create an application that asks for a password, and when the password is correct, opens another file and gives information such as name, age, phone number, etc. As always, I've provided sample code.

```
CLS
10 OPEN "password.txt" for input as #1
20 Input #1, A$
30 Close
40 PRINT "Enter your password!"
50 Input B$
60 If B$=A$ then GOTO 90
70 PRINT "Wrong Password!"
80 GOTO 170
90 OPEN "userdata.txt" for input as #2
100 INPUT #2, name$
110 INPUT #2, age$
120 INPUT #2, color$
130 CLOSE
140 PRINT "Your name is: " + name$
150 PRINT "Your age is: " + age$
160 PRINT "Your favorite color is: " +
color$ + "!"
170 PRINT "End of application!"
```

Debug Me!

```
CLS
10 PRINT "Let's open a file!"
20 OPEN "file.txt" for input #1
30 INPUT #2, A$
40 CLOSE
50 PRINT "Your stored data is: " ; B$
60 PRINT "That's it'
```

Explanation:

Line 20: AS was omitted. Without AS the file will not open.

Line 30: The wrong file number was included here. File #2 doesn't even exist.

Line 50: No B$ variable exists, the declared variable was A$.

Line 60: An apostrophe was inserted instead of a closing quotation mark.

Moral of the Story: Don't omit commands, and always double-check the filename, number, and variable name.

Chapter 5
What do YOU output?

In the last chapter you learned how to get input from a file. But, every time you needed input from a file, you had to first create a file. From my not-too-subtle hints, I'll bet you've already figured out what the next command does. OUTPUT allows you to PRINT to a file.

The same command even allows you to create a file that doesn't already exist! Excited? Read on!

OUTPUT

It seems logical enough, right? The opposite of INPUT is OUTPUT. You'll be happy to know that the OUTPUT command is incredibly similar to the INPUT command.

Both methods below will create new files. There's no need for you to create one by hand! Here's some sample code:

```
OPEN "test.txt" for OUTPUT as #1
PRINT #1, "My output data goes here!"
CLOSE
```

Alternately, you can declare a variable (or get input from the user) to output to a file.

Declared Variable:
```
A$="Your Name"
OPEN "newfile.txt" for OUTPUT as #2
PRINT #2, A$
Close
```

Variable Data from User:
```
PRINT "Type in your name!"
INPUT B$
OPEN "name.txt" for OUTPUT as #3
PRINT #3, B$
CLOSE
```

OUTPUT and Overwriting

Now, I probably should have warned you beforehand, but I'm hoping you've already made this mistake. If you haven't figured it out yet, OUTPUT overwrites anything and everything that you have stored on each file line that you output to.

Like INPUT, you can have multiple OUTPUT's. Each OUTPUT prints a different variable to the file on a different line, to be accessed later by multiple inputs. Brilliant isn't it? BUT, there's the catch I mentioned above. Every OUTPUT overwrites everything on the line you're outputting to. In fact, if you have only one OUTPUT, it overwrites the contents of the entire file.

Using Input and Output Together

So what happens if you want to keep lines 1 and 2 of a file, but want to replace the data in line 3? You're absolutely right! (If you aren't, just pretend.)

You must first OPEN the file for input, INPUT lines 1 and 2 as separate variables, CLOSE the file, OPEN it for output, PRINT variable 1, PRINT variable 2, PRINT variable 3 (this replaces the data in line 3 that you wanted to change!), and finally CLOSE the file. When you think about it, it's a bit like copy and paste in a word processor.

Whew! That's a lot of code to do one simple thing. Now you should be starting to see the complexity that is computer programming. But if it wasn't such a challenge, it wouldn't be so much fun, right?

Here's a bit of sample code demonstrating what I've just described. If you'd like to try this on your own, why not add some lines of code to try creating the file with an output command?

```
10 PRINT "Your pet's name and favorite
chew toy will not change. Please enter
your pet's NEW age below!"
20 INPUT H$
30 OPEN "pet.txt" for INPUT as #1
40 INPUT #1, F$
50 INPUT #1, G$
60 CLOSE
70 OPEN "pet.txt" for OUTPUT as #2
80 PRINT #2, F$
90 PRINT #2, G$
100 PRINT #2, H$
110 CLOSE
```

```
120 PRINT "Your pet's profile has been
updated!"
```

This is just one example of INPUT and OUTPUT being used together. For all other uses, you'll use the same basic code. Be creative and see what you can think of!

Naming INPUTs

Now that you're starting to use a significant number of INPUTs from the USER, I'm going to show you a nifty way to ask the user a question without using the PRINT command on the line before INPUT. This is called an Input Name. Simply type INPUT, your question in quotation marks ("), a comma (,), and finally the variable name. This produces a question on the same line as the input. You may want to put a space after the question to prevent your question from running into the user's typing space. Here's a quick sample:

INPUT "What is your name? ", A$

Alternately, If you like having your question on the line before but just don't like having the ? (in Windows) or the > (in Mac or Linux) to start inputs, you can put empty quotation marks! An example:

INPUT "", B$

A New Trick

Since your applications are starting to get longer, I'm going to show you a little trick to have fewer lines of code. You can insert a colon (:) between different commands and combine the commands onto a single line. This does not result in any visible difference when running your applications, but it makes your code a little cleaner.

Although it's theoretically possible to write all of your commands for a short application onto one line, don't do it. You'll drive yourself insane! Here's an example:

```
CLS:PRINT "Hello!":INPUT "How are you today? ", A$
```

If you'd like to put your comments on the same line as your commands, this is now possible by putting a colon between your command and the comment!

```
PRINT "Hola, amigo!" : 'This prints a greeting.
```

You can even combine all the steps to input from or output to a file:

```
OPEN "test.txt" FOR INPUT AS #1:INPUT #1, A$:CLOSE
```

Pretty sweet, huh?

Short App

You can do some pretty cool stuff now, so write a killer application! I'd like for you to write an application that asks for a password, inputs information and prints it on the screen for the user, and allows the user to update the information on line 4 (or 3 or 5 - anything other than line 1). If you're feeling ambitious, you can add extras: like allowing the user to choose one part of the information to update (you can do it!) or even allowing the user to change the password (with a confirmation input)! I've written a simple application to get you started. It's up to you to add the fun stuff!

```
CLS
10 PRINT "Welcome! Please enter your
password to continue:"
20 Input "Password? ", A$ : 'Asks for
Password
30 OPEN "password.txt" for Input as #1
40 Input #1, B$
50 Close : 'Closes password.txt
60 If A$=B$ then GOTO 80
70 PRINT "Wrong Password! Let's try
again!" : GOTO 20 :'Back to line 20.
80 PRINT "Your name and date of birth will
not be changed. Please enter your updated
telephone number."
90 INPUT C$
100 OPEN "data.txt" for Input as #2
110 Input #2, D$ : 'Gets Name.
120 Input #2, E$ : 'Gets date of birth.
130 Close
```

```
140 OPEN "data.txt" for Output as #3
150 PRINT D$ : 'PRINTs Name.
160 PRINT E$ : 'PRINTs Date of Birth.
170 PRINT C$ : 'This is the updated phone
number!
180 Close
190 PRINT "Thank you for updating your
information!"
```

Debug Me!

```
5 INPUT "Please enter your new favorite
food: ", H$
10 OPEN "file.txt" for OUTPUT as #1
20 INPUT #1, X$
30 INPUT #1, Z$
40 OPEN "file.txt" for OUTPUT as #2
50 PRINT X$
60 PRINT Z$
70 PRINT G$
80 PRINT H$
90 CLOSE
```

Explanation:

Line 10: The file should be opened for INPUT because lines 20 and 30 request input from the file.

Line between 30/40: The CLOSE command was omitted, therefore "file.txt" was never closed.

Line 70: No G$ variable was declared, therefore no G$ variable can be written to the file.

Moral of the Story: Double check to make sure you don't substitute INPUT for OUTPUT or vice-versa, ALWAYS close your files, and keep track of what variables you have and have not declared.

Chapter 6
If it's there, we'll find it!

APPEND

There's one more command you can use to control the data in files. It's the APPEND command. APPEND is used for adding new lines of data to a file. APPEND is like OUTPUT, except it does not overwrite data. The usefulness of APPEND is somewhat limited, but use your imagination! Here's an example of how file data changes with APPEND:

If a file contains the following data,

```
Christopher Anama-Green
Yellow
```

and if I use the APPEND command to add my favorite food to the file, the file now looks like this:

```
Christopher Anama-Green
Yellow
Fried Rice
```

Using the APPEND command is quite similar to using the OUTPUT command, with only one small difference. Here's an example:

```
A$="Fried Rice"
OPEN "thisismylongfilename.txt" for
APPEND as #1
PRINT #1, A$
CLOSE
```

INSTR

You'll find this next command very useful. I have to teach you something useful after dragging you through APPEND. This new command is called INSTR (it's an abbreviation for "in string"). Simply, INSTR is the "search engine" for strings.

You specify the string to search in, the word or phrase you'd like to find, and what happens if the word is found (INSTR is within an IF...THEN command). Here's what the code looks like:

```
IF INSTR (A$, "your word") THEN PRINT "I
found it!"
```

A$ is the string to search in, "your word" is the phrase to search for, and, PRINT is what happens if "your word" is found. Like any IF...THEN command, you can specify any command after THEN (PRINT, GOTO, etc.)

Alternately, you can specify a second variable instead of "your word." This variable can be obtained from user input or file input. Here are examples of both:

```
5 B$="Chris is one cool cat."
10 IF INSTR (B$, "Chris") THEN GOTO 30
20 PRINT "Sorry, no matches found." :
GOTO 40
30 PRINT "I found Chris in the string!"
40 INPUT "Press [enter] to end", D$ :
END
```

Or alternately,

```
5 J$="The quick brown fox jumped over the
lazy dog."
10 INPUT "Enter a word to search for: " A$
20 IF INSTR (J$, A$) THEN GOTO 40
30 Input "No matches found. Press [enter]
to end. ", Z$ : End
40 PRINT "Congrats! Match Found!"
50 Input " Press [enter] to end. ", Y$ :
End
```

If...End If

This is a simple, yet incredibly useful command. This command nests IF...THEN statements within an IF...THEN statement. That means that if and only if one thing is true, several other IF...THEN statements will be tried. The first IF...THEN ends

54

with THEN. That is, no command goes after the first THEN, and the first <u>nested</u> IF...THEN statement goes on the next line. On the line after your last If...Then statement, you put "End If" to end nesting. This may seem a bit complicated until you see it in action. Here's what the code looks like:

```
If favcolor$="green" Then
     If interest$="basketball" then print
"Try NBA.com."
     If interest$="fishing" then print
"Bookmark Fishingworld.com!"
End If

If favcolor$="red" then
     If interest$="shopping" then print
"Go to Amazon.com today!"
     If interest$="knitting" then print
"Visit Knitting.About.com!"
End If
```

Short App

This time we're going to write an FAQ application. You can input data from a file if you'd like, or just store it in the file. Users of your application will be able to type full sentences in question form. You'll use INSTR to search for key words or phrases and IF...THEN nesting to provide answers to questions. I'm not including line numbers in this app, because it makes nesting a bit difficult. Include them if you wish.

```
CLS
PRINT "Welcome to the FAQ app!"
INPUT "What is your computer question? ", A$
CLS

IF INSTR (A$, "mouse") THEN
        If INSTR (A$, "won't move") THEN
PRINT "Is a heavy book on top of your mouse?"
        If INSTR (A$, "looks squashed") THEN
PRINT
    "Did someone sit on it?"
        If INSTR (A$, "won't eat cheese") THEN
    PRINT "All the more cheese for you to enjoy!"
End If

IF INSTR (A$, "keyboard") THEN
        IF INSTR (A$, "dirty") THEN PRINT "Try
Cleaning it!"
        IF INSTR (A$, "ugly") THEN PRINT
"Consider
    painting your keyboard."
        IF INSTR (A$, "won't type") THEN PRINT
"Are you pressing keys hard enough?"
End If

PRINT ""
PRINT "We hope we answered your question in a
 helpful, expedient manner."
INPUT "Press [enter] to end. ", E$ : END
```

Debug Me!

```
IF INSTR (A, "cool") then
        IF INSTR (A$, "beans") THEN PRINT
"Beans are indeed good for your heart."
        IF INSRT (A$, "ice") THEN "Ice makes me
chilly too."
IfEnd
```

Explanation:

Line 1: The A variable should be a string, but is missing $.

Line 4: INSRT should read INSTR. PRINT is omitted. Line should read "...THEN PRINT "Ice makes me..."

Line 6: IfEnd should be End If

Moral of the Story: Remember to assign appropriate names to variables, make sure you don't omit anything, and don't misspell commands.

Chapter 7
Math, Math, Math

Now don't try to skip this chapter because of that dreadful four-letter word (math). I promise, it won't be that bad. You might even have fun!

Declaring Numerical Variables

In Chapter 2, you learned how to declare numerical variables. We haven't used them much since then, so here's a quick review. Numerical variables are declared by typing the variable name (a letter, without an $), an equal sign, and the number (without quotation marks around it). An example:

A=5

Simple Math

First, we're going to learn how to do four simple things with numerical variables. We'll add, subtract, multiply, and divide. These four operations can be completed with two variables from the user, or with a variable from the user and a pre-specified number you program into the code. This is the same basic principle as declaring a string or allowing a user to declare a string.

When adding and subtracting, you'll use the familiar plus (+) and minus (-) signs. For multiplication and division, however you'll use an

asterisk (*) for multiplication and a forward slash
(/) for division.

The actual code is not really anything new. Here are
the four operations:

C=A+B
C=A-B
C=A*B
C=A/B

Here's an example:

```
10 INPUT "Enter the first number: ", A
20 INPUT "Enter the second number: ", B
30 PRINT "Addition:"; A+B
40 PRINT "Subtraction:"; A-B
50 PRINT "Multiplication:"; A*B
60 PRINT "Division:"; A/B
```

Here's another way to do it:

```
10 INPUT "Enter the first number: ", A
20 INPUT "Enter the second number: ", B
30 PRINT "Addition:"
40 C=A+B
50 PRINT C
```

Greater Than, Less Than, Equal To

You've already learned how to set one variable equal to another. Using greater than (>) or less than (<) is as simple. You can also use "greater than or equal to" and "less than or equal to." Below is an example of what these four comparisons look like:

```
A < B
A > B
A <= B
A >= B
```

IF...THEN With Greater Than, Less Than

The utility of greater than/less than is somewhat limited unless combined with an IF...THEN statement. When you put one of these comparisons within an IF...THEN statement though, the result can be incredibly powerful! A greater than or equal to IF...THEN statement might look something like this:

```
IF G >= 100 THEN PRINT "That's pretty
old!"
```

You can combine multiple IF...THEN statements of this sort to provide an appropriate answer depending on the data in the variable.

```
IF G >= 100 THEN PRINT "That's pretty
old!"
IF G <= 100 THEN PRINT "That's still
young!"
```

One problem you may have already spotted with this code is that if G happens to equal 100, both IF...THEN statements are true, and both sentences will be printed. This can be remedied by either including "=" with only one IF...THEN statement, or by adding a colon (:) and a GOTO command after the first.

RND

The last mathematical command I'm going to show you is the RND command. RND is an abbreviation for "random." As you might expect, RND uses the data you input to select a random number. Here's what the full command looks like:

```
Y = INT(RND * var)
```

In the above command, *var* is replaced by a variable or a number. The number replacing var is the "upper limit" (relax, I'm not talking calculus) of the random number selection. In other words, it's the highest possible number that can be selected.

By default, 0 is the lowest number (the "lower limit") that can be selected randomly. To change the lower limit, simply add + and the number to the end of the command.

Here's an example with 2 as the lower limit, and 100 as the upper limit.

```
X = INT(RND * 100) + 2
```

Now, the term "random" is a bit misleading on some counts. You see, if the lower and upper limits are never changed, the same "random" number will be selected every time the program is run. Despite this, when the exact same command with the same upper and lower limits is read multiple times, different random numbers will result.

In short, the only way to make a number truly random is to modify the upper and/or lower limits based on user input.

Here's an example of a simple number guessing game that incorporates user input to select upper and lower limits.

```
CLS
10 INPUT "Enter the highest # I can
pick ", H
20 INPUT "The lowest? ", L
30 N = INT(RND * H) + L
40 CLS
50 INPUT "Guess the number I picked ",
Z
60 IF Z=N THEN GOTO 80
70 PRINT "Wrong! Guess again!" :
GOTO 50
80 PRINT "That's right!"
```

Short App

This time, you're going to create a simple calculator! You can use everything you learned in this chapter to calculate whatever you want: sales tax, savings account growth, you name it! I've created a Miles Per Gallon calculator (feel free to convert to Kilometers Per Liter). Complete source code is below.

```
CLS
10 INPUT "How many miles have you gone
since your last fillup?", M
20 INPUT "How many gallons of gas did
you get at your last fillup?", G
30 CLS
40 T=M/G
50 PRINT "You get: "; T ;"Miles Per
Gallon."
```

Debug Me!

```
CLS
10 PRINT "How many hours have you
worked today?"
20 CLS
30 INPUT A
35 T=8-A
40 IF A > 8 THEN PRINT "You worked ";
T ;" hours overtime.": GOTO 70
50 IF A < 8 THEN PRINT "You worked ";
T ;" too few hours." : GOTO 70
60 PRINT "You worked exactly 8 hours."
70 INPUT, "Press [enter] to end." A$
80 END
```

Explanation:

Line 20: CLS should be removed, as the screen is cleared before the user has time to read line 10.

Line 40: T will be negative, and will not make sense. You must multiply it by –1. T*-1.

Line 70: The comma after input should be removed and placed before A$.

Moral of the Story: Use CLS with care, pay attention to positive and negative numbers, and properly punctuate.

Chapter 8
Leftovers: Loopy stuff

You've reached the last chapter that contains new material! The next four chapters are completely project-based. Congrats on making it this far! In this chapter, I'm going to talk about loops and tie up a few loose ends.

Legal Loops
You've already learned about the infamous "infinite loop." For real applications, infinite loops are still a no-no. However, loops can in fact be very useful and save you a great deal of time typing repetitive code.

I included an incredibly simplified loop in the number guessing game in the last chapter. If you didn't notice it, don't worry. The neon signs didn't arrive in time before publication, otherwise you surely would have noticed it.

Do…Loop
This type of loop repeats a process or command over and over until a specific variable is equal to a number or string predetermined by you.

A "Do…Loop" could be used with a number guessing game. The application would loop until the user correctly guessed the number selected by the application.

Here's what a Do…Loop might look like:

```
DO UNTIL N=969
     INPUT "How old was Methuselah? ", N
LOOP
```

Of course, you can use a string variable instead of a numerical variable:

```
DO UNTIL M$="Methuselah"
     INPUT "Who lived to be 969?", M$
LOOP
```

In the cases above, the program simply ends when the variable is satisfied. Although I only included one command inside the DO…LOOP, you can include as many as you like. I generally add CLS in a situation like this to clean up the screen after each loop cycle.

You can add commands after the DO…LOOP to prompt the user to end the application, etc. You can even add multiple DO…LOOPs one after the other for a quiz-type game.

FOR…NEXT

This is another useful loop method. FOR…NEXT places a limit on the number of loops that can or will occur. Two common uses are inputting a certain number of lines from a file, and placing a limit on the number of times the user can try to enter his or her password.

```
FOR N=1 to 5
     INPUT "What is your favorite
candy?", A$
NEXT N
```

Below is a password example. The user is given 3 tries to get the right password and is reminded how many tries s/he has left.

```
CLS
P=3
FOR N=1 to 3
     CLS
     INPUT "You have ";P;" tries
left: ", A$
     IF A$="password" then GOTO
PassCorrect
     P=P-1
NEXT N

PRINT "I'm sorry. Access denied."
INPUT "Press [enter] to exit. ", G$ :
END

PassCorrect:
PRINT "You got it right!"
INPUT "Press [enter] to exit. ", D$ :
END
```

I know you're excited to see an example of FOR...NEXT in action with file input, so here you go! These few lines of code create a simple text eBook reader application. Try downloading a free book from Project Gutenberg to test this application out.

```
CLS
OPEN "ebook.txt" FOR INPUT AS #1

Start:
FOR N=1 to 20
     INPUT #1, A$
     PRINT A$
NEXT N

INPUT "[enter] to keep reading. 1 to
exit.", G
IF G=1 then END
GOTO Start
```

Last Minute Trick

There is one more little trick I'd like to show you. It can be used with file INPUT or OUTPUT. All code is the same, except for the file name, which is replaced with a (string) variable. The user declares this variable. What all of this means is simply that you can allow users to specify what file the application will open. Useful, aye?

```
INPUT "What file should I open?", A$
OPEN A$ FOR INPUT AS #1
INPUT #1, B$
PRINT B$
CLOSE
```

Tips for Clean Code & Apps

Whether or not you continue to program in BASIC (for all I know, you could end up programming in Java or C), I'd like for you to take away from this book that CLEAN CODE and CLEAN APPS are very, very good!

To write clean code: Always comment your code. Feel free to add spaces and empty lines every now and then. Make use of loops and other timesaving, memory-saving commands. Even if you don't plan on sharing your source code (I shared mine...I'm just saying), you'll find that several months down the road when you decide to look at some old source code, you'll be very thankful you have comments to tell you what's going on.

Making cleaner apps: Clean apps are pretty simple. Vary your colors (if you have that option), use CLS often, include blank lines (PRINT " ") occasionally, don't get too wordy, avoid infinite loops, and finally, don't end your application before users have the opportunity to finish reading the screen! (I almost always prompt-to-end…i.e. INPUT "Press [enter] to end", A$:END)

Short App

This time, I'd like you to create an application that incorporates password protection (using FOR…NEXT) with something that requires DO…LOOP. In the example application I've written below, the user is required to enter a password correctly before taking a short quiz.

```
FOR T=1 to 5
  INPUT "Enter your password: ", A$
  IF A$="password" then GOTO Quiz
Next T
INPUT "Wrong. [enter] to exit.", G$:END

Quiz:
DO UNTIL B$="George Washington"
  Input "Who was the first president? ", B$
Loop

DO UNTIL C$="Samuel"
  INPUT "What's Mark Twain's first name? ", C$
Loop

DO UNTIL D$="Gato"
  INPUT "What is 'cat' in Spanish? ", D$
Loop
```

Debug Me!

```
DO UNTIL G="5"
   INPUT "How many fingers do I have?", G
NEXT

DO UNTIL D$="password"
   INPUT "Enter your password: ", D
LOOP
```

Explanation:

Line 3: NEXT was inserted instead of LOOP.

Line 5: Input for D is requested. D is numerical variable and can't be used for a password. The loop is only satisfied when D$ equals "password." If the variables do not match, the loop will never be satisfied, resulting in an infinite loop.

Moral of the Story: Remember what type of loop you're using, always double-check variable names, and make sure you don't accidentally include infinite loops.

Chapter 9

Project 1: Money Manager

These last four chapters will be a bit different, as they're entirely project-based. You should now know enough to write these projects entirely on your own! But don't worry, I'm not going to turn you loose without any guidance. Each project includes example code.

Money Manager

Money: it's on everyone's mind, right? (Really unfortunate, but that's a different book altogether.) What better way to make use of BASIC mathematical operations than to make a money manager?

There's no limit to what you can do with this project. As always, I've created a sample application for you. I've simply started you off with a sales tax calculator and a "monthly gas budget" calculator. You can add as many more as you'd like. If you're feeling really ambitious, why not combine several calculators to make a nice full-budget application?

The next example includes all of the code for this application. Following the code, I've explained the simple equations in the application.

```
CLS
10 PRINT "Welcome to Money Manager."
20 PRINT ""
30 PRINT "1) Gas Budget Calculator"
40 PRINT "2) Sales Tax Calculator"
45 PRINT "3) Exit"
50 INPUT "The # of your choice: ", A
60 IF A=1 then GOTO 90
70 IF A=2 then GOTO 170
75 IF A=3 then END
80 CLS: PRINT "Invalid entry.": GOTO
30
90 CLS: PRINT "Gas Budget Calculator":
PRINT ""
100 INPUT "How much can you spend on
gas per week? ", S
110 INPUT "How much is gas per gallon?
", G
120 INPUT "How many MPG do you
average? ", M
130 C=S/G : T=C*M : CLS
140 PRINT "You can travel: "; T
;"miles this week."
150 INPUT "[enter] to return to
menu.", G$
160 CLS: GOTO 10

170 CLS: PRINT "Sales Tax Calculator"
180 PRINT ""
190 INPUT "Enter the price of the
item: ", P
200 INPUT "Enter your state sales tax
in %: ", Z
210 H=Z/100 : L=P*H : W=P+L
```

```
220 CLS: PRINT "You will pay $";L;"in
tax for a total of: $";W;"!"
230 INPUT "[enter] to return to menu.
", H$
240 CLS: GOTO 10
```

Program Breakdown

Gas Budget Calculator:
Initially, the user is asked how much he would like to spend on gas per week (S declared).

Next, the user declares the price of gas per gallon (G).

Finally, the user enters his vehicle's average MPG (M).

The app completes a series of simple calculations that may look daunting at first, but are really quite simple.

C=S/G. First, a new variable (C) must be declared by the app. C is equal to $$ spend per week (S) divided by price of gas per gallon (G). This provides the number of gallons the user will be able to buy (C).

T=C*M. Next, another new variable (T) is declared by the app. T equals the number of gallons (C) the user can buy times the user's average miles per gallon (M). The result is the total number of miles the user can drive by paying (S) amount of money for (C) gallons of gas.

Sales Tax Calculator:
First, the user declares the price of the item (P).
Lastly, the user declares the state sales tax in % (Z).

$H=Z/100$. H is declared by the app. H is the sales tax in % divided by 100, or the sales tax per dollar.

$L=P*H$. The next new variable is L. L is equal to the price of the item (P) times the sales tax per dollar (H). More simply, L is the total sales tax paid by the user for (P) item.

$W=P+L$. This final equation declares W, or the total price including sales tax. W is equal to the price of the item (P) plus the total sales tax for the item (L).

Chapter 10
Project 2: Address Book

The money manager wasn't so bad, was it? This second project is a simple address book. I say simple, because I've only included space for names and phone numbers. It's up to you to add postal addresses, e-mail addresses, and anything else you can think of! The possibilities are endless.

Address Book

This address book makes extensive use of loops and file commands. I mostly used APPEND here to save repeated INPUTs and OUTPUTs. The downside of sticking with APPEND is that there's no edit or delete capability for entries. However, it's entirely possible to add these two capabilities using what you know. (Hint: You may find it helpful to create a separate "temp file" to copy from and paste to.)

Ordinarily, an application like this would be accomplished with simple databases. However, databases are a bit beyond the scope of this book, so we'll be sticking with plain old bread and butter text files. *As an aside: if you would like to learn more about BASIC databases, I highly recommend the tutorials published online at www.qbasic.com.*

```
CLS
10  PRINT "Address Book"
20  PRINT ""
30  PRINT "1) Search Entries"
40  PRINT "2) Add Entry"
45  PRINT "3) Exit"
50  INPUT "Enter the # of your choice:
", C
60  IF C=1 THEN GOTO 90
70  IF C=2 THEN GOTO 180
75  IF C=3 THEN END
80  CLS: PRINT "Invalid Entry.": GOTO
30

90  CLS: INPUT "Enter a name or number:
", H$
100 OPEN "total.txt" FOR INPUT as #1
105 INPUT #1, T: close
110 OPEN "data.txt" for INPUT as #10
120 Z=1:I=0
130 FOR Z=1 TO T
      INPUT #10, R$
      IF INSTR(R$, H$) THEN PRINT
R$:I=1
140 Next Z
150 CLOSE
160 IF I=1 THEN INPUT "End of results.
[enter] to return to menu. ", J$: CLS:
GOTO 10
170 INPUT "No results found. ", J$:
CLS: GOTO 10

180 CLS: INPUT "Enter new name: ", N$
190 INPUT "Enter phone #: ", P$
200 OPEN "total.txt" FOR INPUT as #2
```

```
210 INPUT #2, U
220 CLOSE
230 OPEN "data.txt" for APPEND as #3
240 PRINT #3, N$; " | "; P$
250 CLOSE
260 OPEN "total.txt" for OUTPUT as #4
270 PRINT #4, U+1
280 CLOSE
290 CLS: INPUT "Entry added. [enter]
to return to menu.", W$: CLS: GOTO 10
```

Program Breakdown

First and foremost, you must create two text files.
Call the first "total.txt." Open it, enter "1" on the
first line, save it, and close it. The second file should
be called "data.txt." Open it, enter some jargon on
the first line (anything you'd like, really), save it,
and close it.

Total.txt keeps track of how many entries are saved,
and data.txt records all entries, one entry per line.

The way this app works is relatively simple. We'll
start with the search function.

Search:
The user enters a name or number to search for. The
app first opens total.txt to find out how many times
it can INPUT from data.txt (variable T), and then
proceeds to do just that. File INPUT from data.txt is

accomplished with a FOR...NEXT loop, with the end point being the value of total.txt (variable T: how many entries are in data.txt = how many lines are in data.txt = how many inputs from data.txt).

As matching (even partial matches) entries are found, they will be printed onto the screen.

Finally, I is an important, but easily overlooked, variable in this application. I is first declared as 0 and is only changed (to 1) if at least one match for the user's search term (H$) is found. Near the end of the SEARCH section, if I=1 (a match has been found), the program can respond appropriately with "No matches found" or "End of results."

Add Entry:
Adding entries is a bit simpler than searching for entries.

First, total.txt is opened to see how many lines are in data.txt (U is declared).

Next, data.txt is opened for APPEND. The new entry is printed on a new line in data.txt using the format Name (N$) | Number (P$). You can change the format to suit yourself, or better yet, add an option for users to select which format they'd like to use!

Finally, total.txt is re-opened, this time for OUTPUT, and U + 1 (the value originally retrieved from total.txt, plus 1) is printed to the file.

Chapter 11
Project 3: BMI Calculator

This project focuses on something we could all use a little more of – no, not money – health! As Virgil said, "The greatest wealth is health." But enough philosophy...let's get started.

We've all heard about the "obesity epidemic." If you live in the Western hemisphere, chances are you or someone you know may be overweight or obese. But how do we measure when someone is "overweight" or "obese?"

We use the Body Mass Index measure or BMI for short. BMI takes height and weight, and calculates BMI. This number can then be compared to established ranges for underweight, normal weight, overweight, and obese.

BMI Calculator
The actual BMI equation is pretty simple. For metric, replace pounds with kg and inches with cm.

BMI = Weight lbs. **/** (Height in. **x** Height in.) **x** 703

A BASIC equation might look something like this, where B is for BMI, W is for weight, and H is for height:

$$B = (W/(H*H))*703$$

Or, you can break the equation down into parts, where X, Y, and Z are arbitrary variable names that can be replaced with your own:

$$X = H*H$$
$$Y = W/X$$
$$Z = Y*703$$

You may want to view a sample BMI calculator or two online to get ideas about how to construct one of your own.

```
CLS
10 PRINT "BMI Calculator"
20 PRINT ""
30 PRINT "Please enter your weight, in
pounds."
40 INPUT W
50 PRINT "Please enter your height, in
inches."
60 INPUT H
70 B = (W/(H*H))*703
80 b$ = "normal"
90 if B <= 18.5 then b$="underweight"
100 if B >= 25 then b$="overweight"
110 if B >= 30 then b$="obese"
120 PRINT "Your BMI is: ";B;" which is
in the ";b$;" range."
```

Program Breakdown

First we ask for the user's weight and height. These items are then used to calculate BMI using the standard equation.

Then, we compare the BMI to established values for different BMI ranges. BMI of less than 18.5 is considered underweight; 18.5-24.9 is normal weight; 25-29.9 is overweight; and 30 or above is obese.

The program then prints out the calculated BMI and the corresponding weight range.

One consideration that this program does not make is adjustment for gender. To get the most accurate BMI calculation, there are some minor adjustments and considerations for gender and age – you may want to do a little research and adjust your code to make your program more robust!

Chapter 12

Project 4: Chatbot

If you ever spent time on AOL Instant Messenger with SmarterChild or online with ALICE bot, you've talked to chatbots before. Likely, you've talked with lots of chatbots whether or not you realize it. Often when you call customer service and are asked to give "voice responses" to a computer, you're chatting with a chatbot. A well-designed chatbot is a basic form of artificial intelligence.

In our final project, you're going to use <u>everything</u> you've learned to create your very own command line BASIC chat bot. You can make this as simple or as complicated as you wish. The more vocabulary words you add and define, the more interesting your bot will be to chat with.

As you practice coding and chatting with your bot, you'll see that it's best to program your bot with more general answers – that way the bot will have a better chance of answering appropriately to questions posed or statements made by the user.

The core command that you will use is one from earlier in the book:

```
IF INSTR("some text", A$) THEN
```

This allows the bot to scan questions and statements posed by the user and search for key words or phrases and then respond appropriately.

If you'd like, you can make a chatbot limited to a particular topic – that will definitely make the process easier. You could make a mathematical chatbot that makes math a bit more fun. Of if you're fluent in more than one language...try making a bot than can recognize greetings in different languages and respond appropriately. Or, to simplify, you can add a few chatbot-like features to any other program that you have created to create a friendly/customized atmosphere.

The possibilities are endless!

Here are a few lines of sample code for a chatbot named Thom to get you started...good luck!

```
10 CLS
20 INPUT "Hello! I am Thom. What is
      your name? ", A$
30 PRINT "Nice to meet you, "; A$
40 INPUT "Where are you from? ", B$
50 PRINT "I hear "; B$; " is lovely.
60 INPUT "Ask me anything! ", C$

70 If INSTR (C$, "how") THEN PRINT "I
      am fine, thanks. How about
      you?": GOTO 60
```

```
80 If INSTR (C$, "fine") THEN PRINT
      "Glad to hear it!": GOTO 60

90 If INSTR (C$, "bye") THEN GOTO 1000

100 If INSTR (C$, "what's up") THEN
      PRINT "The sky! Taxes! My blood
      pressure!": GOTO 60

900 Print "Hmm I am not understanding
      you. Could you ask something
      else?": GOTO 60

1000 PRINT "Great chatting with you,
      "; A$; ". See ya!": END
```

As you can see from the code above, after every answer the user is referred back to the same question "Ask me anything!" This can be changed to accommodate whatever you like – but as mentioned earlier, it's good to be general.

With this code you can nest IF…THEN statements if you so choose. It would work well to nest question words like WHO, WHAT, WHEN with other words that make it easier to predict the kind of question the user is asking.

Afterword

Congratulations on your newly acquired computer programming skills! I've no doubt that you're already well on your way to becoming a fine BASIC computer programmer.

You can continue to program in BASIC, or you may wish to try Visual BASIC or REALbasic. You'll be amazed how similar the BASIC you know is to these descendants on the evolutionary BASIC tree.

Should you choose to continue programming in BASIC, consider purchasing the full version of FirstBasic (it's cheap, and well worth the cost) if you're running Windows, or take a look at METAL BASIC if you're running Mac OS (9 or X). METAL BASIC is by far one of the best BASIC compilers I've ever used, and it's free!

Whether you remain a hobbyist programmer, or end up as a software engineer, thank you for making *Command Line BASIC* part of your programming journey.

Acknowledgments

A big thank you goes to the makers of Metal BASIC (the best Mac OS BASIC compiler on the planet, in my opinion), FirstBasic (again, an excellent and affordable DOS/Windows compiler), and of course Chipmunk BASIC/HotPaw BASIC (the interpreter I used to learn BASIC).

Thank you to Qbasic.com for teaching me, many years ago, about file input/output and legal loops. Qbasic.com is one of the best BASIC resources available on the Internet.

Last but not least, I'd like to thank the authors of the vintage children's BASIC programming books that I used to start learning BASIC. I would have been lost without them in my attempts to write my first program many years ago.

www.ingramcontent.com/pod-product-compliance
Lightning Source LLC
Chambersburg PA
CBHW031227050326
40689CB00009B/1509